THE WEALTH TRAIN

DAVID MARK

DEDICATION

In dedication to those who believe in the power of purposeful actions, tireless perseverance, and unwavering commitment. May **'The Wealth Train'** be your compass through the financial landscapes, navigating you toward prosperity's shores and illuminating the path to lasting abundance and fulfillment. This book stands as a tribute to your aspirations, igniting the flames of possibility and guiding you to harness the boundless potential within.

ACKNOWLEDGMENTS

To the mentors whose wisdom shaped my understanding and the experiences that sculpted my perspective. 'The Wealth Train' is a mosaic of lessons learned, gratitude owed, and insights gained. Each page is a tribute to the invaluable guidance received and the invaluable experiences lived, steering us toward a world where knowledge breeds prosperity and every lesson leads to wealth.

TABLE OF CONTENTS

INTRODUCTION

In a world pulsating with aspirations for financial independence and prosperity, **'The Wealth Train'** emerges as more than a mere guide; it stands as a testament to the enduring pursuit of abundance in every facet of life. Imagine a journey where each chapter unfolds like a new landscape, revealing the secrets, strategies, and transformative power that lead to financial freedom.

As the locomotive of this expedition, ***'The Wealth Train'*** chugs along the tracks of economic, financial and global landscapes, offering a panoramic view of the principles, tactics, and mindset necessary to navigate the complex terrains of wealth accumulation and sustainability. It's an odyssey woven with the threads of experience, insight, and relentless determination, crafted to empower, educate, and elevate every passenger willing to embark on this transformative voyage.

This is not just another financial manual; it's a beacon illuminating the pathways to prosperity considering the global phase of change which we are experiencing. Through the windows of these pages, the reader gazes upon the rich tapestry of knowledge, fortified by the lessons drawn from the successes, failures, and wisdom of titans in the realm of wealth creation.

From the foundational pillars of financial literacy to the intricacies of investment strategies, 'The Wealth

Train' offers a comprehensive itinerary for the expedition towards financial empowerment. It delves into the psychological landscapes that shape our relationship with money, unravels the mysteries of risk and reward, and empowers individuals with the tools to engineer not just robust but a sustainable financial future.

The engine that propels this train isn't just information; it's a transformative force, fueled by the stories, experiences and secrets of those who have traversed the tumultuous yet rewarding paths to wealth. It's an anthology of triumphs and setbacks, a compilation of wisdom distilled from the experiences of trailblazers who have mastered the art of wealth accumulation.

Prepare to board this locomotive of enlightenment, where each chapter unveils a treasure trove of insights, propelling you toward financial sovereignty. 'The Wealth Train' beckons—a journey of self-discovery, empowerment, and the realization of boundless potential awaits. All aboard as we embark on this transformative expedition towards a life of prosperity and fulfillment.
rations.

1

CHAPTER ONE

SETTING THE FOUNDATION

DEFINING WEALTH

Wealth is the destination and the journey aboard the intricate tracks of financial freedom. It mirrors the landscape seen from the windows of a speeding train—a panorama of possibilities, opportunities, and acquisitions.

On this journey, wealth is the locomotive that propels us toward financial sovereignty. It's the security of a well-structured plan and the momentum gained from strategic investments. Like the rhythm of a train's wheels on the tracks, wealth resonates with the steady growth of assets and the momentum of compound interest.

It's not solely about amassed fortunes; rather, wealth encompasses the freedom the train ride affords—freedom from financial constraints, from the worries of debt, and from the shackles of uncertainty. It's the confidence to switch tracks, take calculated risks, and explore new avenues.

Much like a train journey, wealth is both a voyage and a destination. It's the thrill of progress along the tracks of diversified portfolios and the eventual arrival at the platform of financial independence.

The compartments of this wealth train are filled not only with tangible assets but also with intangible riches. It's the freedom to spend time with loved ones, the joy of pursuing passions, and the peace of mind that comes with a secure financial future.

Ultimately, wealth on this journey is the synergy between fiscal abundance and the liberty it provides—a journey where each stop along the way, each investment made, brings one closer to the horizon of financial freedom.

CULTIVATING A WEALTH MINDSET

Cultivating a wealth mindset is akin to nurturing fertile soil for the seeds of prosperity to thrive. It extends beyond financial acumen, delving into the very fabric of thoughts, beliefs, and perspectives. At its core lies an embrace of the abundance mentality, a shift from scarcity thinking towards a worldview where opportunities abound, and success is within reach for those willing to pursue it. This shift serves as a catalyst, unlocking boundless creativity and resourcefulness that fuel the journey toward wealth.

Central to this mindset shift is the cultivation of a growth-oriented approach. This entails viewing challenges as opportunities for learning and personal development. Rather than allowing setbacks to deter progress, individuals with a wealth mindset perceive them as stepping stones toward growth, continuously evolving and adapting to their environment.

Moreover, fostering a wealth mindset involves nurturing a positive self-image and belief in one's ability to achieve financial success. Confidence and self-worth become cornerstones, allowing individuals to embrace opportunities and navigate financial endeavors with conviction and resilience. Alongside this, cultivating a clear vision of financial goals becomes imperative. This vision acts as a guiding beacon, providing direction and focus amid the complexities of wealth creation.

Emotional intelligence plays a pivotal role in this journey. Understanding the interplay between emotions and financial decisions is crucial. Cultivating the ability to make rational choices in the face of emotional impulses ensures sound financial planning and execution. Additionally, the practice of mindfulness and gratitude intertwines with this mindset. Gratitude for existing resources fosters a sense of abundance, while mindfulness guides prudent financial decisions.

Collaboration and networking also feature prominently in cultivating a wealth mindset. Building relationships with like-minded individuals, mentors, and supportive networks not only provides valuable guidance but also opens doors to collective wisdom and resources. This interconnectedness amplifies opportunities and accelerates the path toward wealth.

In essence, A train cannot deliver its purpose without its track in the same vain our mindsets should be restructured in a way that it can convey us to our desired destination of wealth. Cultivating a wealth mindset transcends financial literacy; it involves a fundamental shift in perspective. It's an ongoing journey of mindset refinement, empowering individuals to harness the power of their thoughts, beliefs, and actions as catalysts for sustained wealth creation.

IDENTIFYING YOUR FINANCIAL GOAL

Identifying financial goals serves as the compass guiding one's journey toward wealth creation. It's the process of envisioning, defining, and prioritizing objectives that align with one's aspirations and desired lifestyle. To embark on this journey effectively, several key steps and considerations are essential.

Clarity and Specificity: Defining financial goals begins with clarity. It involves articulating specific and measurable objectives. Whether it's achieving a certain level of savings, clearing debts, investing in property, or planning for retirement, specificity provides a clear target to work towards.

Short-Term and Long-Term Vision:

Delineating between short-term and long-term financial goals is crucial. Short-term goals might encompass immediate needs like creating an emergency fund or paying off credit card debt, while long-term goals could involve retirement planning, investments, or wealth accumulation for future generations.

Realistic and Achievable: While aiming high is commendable, setting realistic goals is imperative. Financial goals should be challenging yet attainable within a reasonable timeframe. Realism ensures motivation remains high, preventing discouragement from unattainable objectives.

Alignment with Values and Priorities: Each individual's financial goals are unique and should reflect personal values and priorities. Whether it's a focus on experiences, family security, philanthropy, or personal growth, aligning goals with values adds purpose and motivation to the pursuit of wealth.

Quantifiable Metrics: Establishing quantifiable metrics aids in tracking progress and measuring success. This involves setting specific milestones and timelines, allowing for regular assessment and adjustment of strategies to stay on course.

Risk Appetite and Time Horizon: Understanding one's risk tolerance and time horizon is essential. Some goals may require more aggressive investment strategies, while others may necessitate a more conservative approach, depending on individual preferences and timeframes.

Regular Review and Adaptation: Financial goals are not static; they evolve over time. Regularly reviewing and reassessing goals ensures they remain relevant and aligned with changing circumstances, allowing for adaptation as life circumstances or priorities shift.

In essence, identifying financial goals is a deliberate and introspective process. It involves introspection, planning, and the conscious alignment of aspirations with actionable objectives. By setting clear, achievable, and personally meaningful goals, individuals lay the groundwork for a purposeful and effective journey toward financial abundance and fulfillment.

2

CHAPTER TWO

MANAGING YOUR FINANCES

BUDGETING AND SAVING STRATEGIES

Budgeting and saving strategies are the cornerstones of financial stability and wealth accumulation. They form the scaffolding upon which successful financial plans are built. Adopting effective budgeting and saving practices involves a combination of discipline, strategy, and prudent decision-making.

Establishing a Comprehensive Budget: The foundation of effective financial management is creating a comprehensive budget. This involves meticulously outlining income sources and categorizing expenses, including necessities, discretionary spending, and savings goals. A budget serves as a roadmap, guiding spending patterns and ensuring financial alignment with goals.

Embracing the 50/30/20 Rule: An effective guideline for budgeting involves allocating 50% of income to essentials like housing, utilities, and groceries, 30% to discretionary spending such as entertainment, dining out, and 20% to savings and debt repayment. This rule provides structure while allowing flexibility in managing finances.

Prioritizing Saving and Automating it: Cultivating a habit of saving is fundamental. Setting aside a portion of income for savings as a non-negotiable expense reinforces financial discipline. Automating savings through direct deposits or transfers ensures consistency and reduces the temptation to spend before saving.

Emergency Fund and Contingency Planning: Building an emergency fund is pivotal. Allocating funds for unexpected expenses or financial emergencies provides a safety net, preventing the need to dip into long-term savings or incur debt during challenging times.

Debt Management and Reduction: Strategically managing and reducing debt is crucial. Prioritizing high-interest debts while making consistent payments toward lowering outstanding balances helps free up resources for savings and investments.

Evaluating and Adjusting Spending Habits: Regularly evaluating spending habits allows for identifying areas where adjustments can be made. It involves distinguishing between needs and wants, cutting unnecessary expenses, and reallocating funds towards savings or investment goals.

Harnessing Technology and Tools: Utilizing budgeting apps or financial tools simplifies tracking expenses, monitoring progress, and staying accountable to budgetary goals. These tools offer insights into spending patterns and facilitate informed financial decisions.

Incremental Increases in Savings: As income grows or expenses decrease, consider gradually increasing savings contributions. Incremental increases ensure lifestyle adjustments are manageable while steadily enhancing savings capacity.

Consistency and Persistence: Consistency is key to successful budgeting and saving. Maintaining discipline, persistently adhering to budgetary guidelines, and regularly revisiting and refining strategies reinforce financial health.

By implementing these strategies, individuals can fortify their financial foundation, cultivate healthy saving habits, and navigate towards achieving their short-term and long-term financial goals. Effective budgeting and saving not only secure financial stability but also lay the groundwork for wealth accumulation and long-term prosperity.

DEBT MANAGEMENT AND ELIMINATION

Debt management and elimination stand as pivotal components on the path to financial freedom. Addressing and effectively handling debts not only alleviate financial burdens but also create opportunities for wealth accumulation. Here are key considerations and strategies for managing and eliminating debts:

Comprehensive Assessment: Initiating debt management begins with a thorough assessment of all outstanding debts. This includes categorizing debts by interest rates, outstanding balances, and payment schedules. Understanding the full scope of indebtedness serves as a foundation for devising a strategic plan.

Prioritization and Organization: Prioritizing debts based on interest rates, known as the "debt avalanche" method, or focusing on smaller debts first, known as the "debt snowball" method, aids in developing an effective repayment strategy. Organizing debts allows for systematic and targeted repayment efforts.

Budgeting and Expense Evaluation: Establishing a realistic budget is fundamental. It involves a comprehensive evaluation of expenses to identify areas where spending can be reduced or reallocated toward debt repayment. Creating a disciplined budget ensures consistent allocation of funds towards debt elimination.

Negotiation and Consolidation: Exploring opportunities for negotiation with creditors for lower interest rates or more favorable repayment terms can significantly aid debt management. Additionally, debt consolidation, combining multiple debts into a single payment with a lower interest rate, can streamline repayments and reduce overall interest costs.

Increased Income and Additional Payments: Supplementing income through side hustles, part-time work, or selling unused assets can accelerate debt repayment. Allocating any additional income or windfalls directly towards debt payments expedites the elimination process.

Financial Discipline and Lifestyle Adjustments: Cultivating financial discipline by avoiding new debt and making conscious lifestyle adjustments helps prevent further accumulation of debts. These adjustments might involve cutting unnecessary expenses or finding more cost-effective alternatives.

Seeking Professional Guidance: In complex debt situations or when overwhelmed, seeking guidance from financial advisors or debt counselors can provide tailored strategies and insights. They can offer personalized advice on debt management, negotiation, and long-term financial planning.

Regular Monitoring and Celebrating Progress: Consistently monitoring debt reduction progress helps stay motivated and focused. Celebrating milestones along the way reinforces positive financial behaviors and keeps individuals engaged in the debt elimination journey.

Effectively managing and eliminating debt requires commitment, discipline, and a strategic approach. By implementing these strategies and adopting a proactive mindset towards debt, individuals can pave the way towards financial freedom, laying a solid foundation for future wealth-building endeavors.

INVESTMENT BASICS: BUILDING YOUR PORTFOLIO

Building an investment portfolio is akin to constructing a sturdy edifice: it requires a solid foundation, diversified materials, and a blueprint that aligns with one's financial goals and risk tolerance. The fundamentals of building a portfolio encompass several key elements:

Understanding Risk and Return: A foundational principle involves comprehending the relationship between risk and return. Investments typically entail varying levels of risk, and higher potential returns often accompany higher risk. Balancing these factors is crucial when constructing a portfolio.

Asset Allocation: Diversification across different asset classes—such as stocks, bonds, real estate, and commodities—reduces overall risk. The proportion of each asset class in a portfolio should align with an individual's risk tolerance, time horizon, and financial objectives.

Risk Tolerance and Time Horizon: Assessing one's risk tolerance and time horizon is pivotal. Younger investors with a longer time horizon might opt for more aggressive growth-oriented investments, while those closer to retirement might prioritize more conservative, income-focused assets.

Research and Due Diligence: Conducting thorough research before investing is imperative. Understanding the fundamentals of potential investments, evaluating their historical performance, and considering market trends and economic indicators aids in making informed decisions.

Diversification within Asset Classes: Even within a specific asset class, diversification is key. For instance, within stocks, spreading investments across various industries, company sizes, and geographical regions helps mitigate specific risks associated with individual stocks.

Regular Review and Rebalancing: Portfolios require periodic review and rebalancing. As market conditions and investment performances fluctuate, rebalancing ensures the portfolio remains aligned with the desired asset allocation and financial objectives.

Costs and Fees: Being mindful of investment costs and fees is essential. High fees can significantly impact overall returns, so selecting low-cost investment options, such as index funds or exchange-traded funds (ETFs), can be advantageous.

Staying Informed and Seeking Guidance: Staying informed about market trends, economic indicators, and financial news is beneficial. Seeking advice from financial professionals or advisors can also provide valuable insights and guidance in portfolio construction and management.

Building an investment portfolio is a dynamic process, requiring a blend of strategy, discipline, and adaptability. By adhering to these investment basics, individuals can construct portfolios that not only align with their financial objectives but also navigate the complexities of the financial markets more effectively.

3

CHAPTER THREE

GROWING YOUR WEALTH

ADVANCED INVESTMENT STRATEGIES

Advanced investment strategies are like tools in the hands of seasoned artisans, offering ways to optimize wealth growth through sophisticated techniques. These strategies, while not without risks, can potentially yield higher returns for those willing to navigate the complexities of the financial markets. Here are some advanced investment strategies:

1. Alternative Investments: These encompass a wide range of assets beyond traditional stocks and bonds. Examples include private equity, hedge funds, venture capital, real estate, commodities, and derivatives. These investments often offer diversification and the potential for higher returns but may involve higher risk and less liquidity.

2. Leveraging: Leveraging involves using borrowed funds to amplify investment returns. Margin trading in stocks or utilizing leverage in real estate investments can magnify gains, but it also increases exposure to losses, making it a high-risk strategy that requires careful consideration and risk management.

3. Options and Derivatives: Options trading involves contracts that give the holder the right to buy or sell assets at predetermined prices within a specified time frame. Derivatives, such as futures or swaps, derive their value from an underlying asset. These complex financial instruments can be used for hedging or speculative purposes but require a deep understanding of market dynamics and carry inherent risks.

4. Sector Rotation and Tactical Asset Allocation: These strategies involve dynamically shifting investments between different sectors or asset classes based on market conditions or economic indicators. By actively managing portfolio allocations, investors aim to capitalize on short-term opportunities and protect against downturns.

5. Arbitrage Strategies: Arbitrage involves exploiting price discrepancies of the same asset across different markets. This can include geographical arbitrage, where assets are bought in one market and sold in another for a profit due to pricing inefficiencies.

6. High-Frequency Trading and Algorithmic Trading: Utilizing advanced technology and algorithms, these strategies involve executing trades at incredibly high speeds based on predefined parameters. While potentially profitable, they require sophisticated infrastructure, technical expertise, and constant monitoring.

7. Tax-Efficient Investing: Strategies like tax-loss harvesting, where investment losses are used to offset gains, and employing tax-advantaged accounts or structures can optimize after-tax returns, enhancing overall wealth growth.

Navigating these advanced strategies requires a deep understanding of financial markets, risk management, and often specialized knowledge. It's crucial to approach these strategies with caution and consider factors such as risk tolerance, investment goals, and the expertise required for implementation.

Moreover, diversification remains a fundamental principle even within advanced strategies. While these techniques offer potential for higher returns, they also come with increased complexity and risks. Consulting with financial advisors or professionals experienced in these strategies can provide invaluable guidance and help mitigate potential pitfalls. Advanced strategies should align with an investor's financial goals and risk tolerance, forming part of a comprehensive investment plan rather than standalone approaches.

REAL ESTATE AND ALTERNATIVE INVESTMENTS

Real estate and alternative investments present compelling avenues for growing wealth, offering diverse opportunities beyond traditional investment vehicles like stocks and bonds. These asset classes often provide unique advantages, including potential for consistent returns, diversification, and tangible asset ownership.

Real Estate Investments:
Residential Properties: Investing in residential real estate involves purchasing properties like single-family homes, apartments, or condominiums for rental income or capital appreciation. It offers steady cash flow through rental income and the potential for property value appreciation over time.

Commercial Properties: Commercial real estate, including office buildings, retail spaces, and warehouses, presents opportunities for higher returns. Leasing space to businesses generates rental income, and these properties often have longer lease terms, providing stability and potential for higher yields.

Real Estate Investment Trusts (REITs): REITs are publicly traded companies that own and manage income-generating real estate portfolios. Investing in REITs allows individuals to access real estate markets without owning physical properties directly. They provide liquidity, diversification, and the potential for dividends.

Real Estate Crowdfunding: This modern investment avenue allows investors to pool funds to invest in real estate projects. Through online platforms, individuals can participate in various real estate deals, such as residential developments or commercial properties, with lower capital requirements.

Alternative Investments:

Private Equity: Private equity investments involve buying equity in privately-held companies. These investments can be lucrative but typically require significant capital and are illiquid, as they often involve holding the investment for an extended period before realizing returns.

Venture Capital: Investing in early-stage companies with high growth potential characterizes venture capital. While inherently risky, successful investments in startups can yield substantial returns if the companies grow or undergo lucrative exits, such as acquisitions or IPOs.

Hedge Funds: Hedge funds pool capital from multiple investors and employ various strategies to generate returns. They often have more flexibility in investment options and can use strategies such as leveraging and short-selling. However, they are typically limited to accredited investors due to their complex nature and higher risk profile.

Commodities and Precious Metals: Investing in commodities like gold, silver, or oil can serve as a hedge against inflation and market volatility. Precious metals, in particular, have historically been a store of value during economic uncertainties.

Real estate and alternative investments can diversify portfolios, potentially providing higher returns and hedging against market volatility. However, they often require careful due diligence, understanding of market dynamics, and sometimes higher capital commitments. Engaging with experienced professionals and thoroughly researching opportunities are essential steps in harnessing the potential of these investment avenues for wealth growth.

CULTIVATING A WEALTH MINDSET

Entrepreneurship stands as a potent avenue for wealth creation, embodying the spirit of innovation, risk-taking, and vision. It's a journey that transcends conventional employment, offering individuals the opportunity to create value, solve problems, and potentially amass substantial wealth. The relationship between entrepreneurship and wealth creation is multifaceted and rooted in various key aspects:

Creating Value and Solving Problems: At its core, entrepreneurship revolves around identifying unmet needs or inefficiencies in the market and devising innovative solutions. Successful entrepreneurs focus on creating value for their customers or society, often leading to the establishment of profitable businesses.

Opportunity for Unlimited Growth: Unlike traditional employment, where income might have limits, entrepreneurship offers the potential for limitless growth. Successful ventures can scale rapidly, leading to exponential wealth accumulation.

Risk and Reward: Entrepreneurship inherently involves risk-taking. While it comes with the possibility of failure, it also presents the opportunity for substantial rewards. The willingness to take calculated risks and learn from failures is integral to the entrepreneurial journey.

Ownership and Control: Entrepreneurs have the autonomy to shape their ventures, owning the outcomes and having control over strategic decisions. This ownership often translates into substantial financial rewards as businesses succeed and grow.

Innovation and Adaptability: Entrepreneurs thrive on innovation and adaptability. They constantly seek new opportunities, adapt to changing market dynamics, and innovate to stay ahead of the curve, fostering an environment conducive to wealth creation.

Building Assets and Equity: Successful entrepreneurs build valuable assets and equity through their businesses. As ventures grow, so does the value of their ownership stake, contributing significantly to their overall wealth.

Job Creation and Economic Impact: Entrepreneurship not only creates wealth for individuals but also generates employment opportunities, fosters economic growth, and contributes to the overall prosperity of communities.

However, it's important to note that entrepreneurship isn't a guaranteed path to wealth. It requires dedication, resilience, and a willingness to learn from both successes and failures. Many ventures face challenges and obstacles, and success often requires perseverance through difficult times.

Furthermore, while entrepreneurship offers significant potential for wealth creation, it's not the only route. Diversification of income streams, prudent investment strategies, and financial discipline are equally important in building sustainable wealth.

In summary, entrepreneurship stands as a powerful catalyst for wealth creation, offering individuals the opportunity to build substantial wealth through innovation, perseverance, and the creation of value in the marketplace.

4

CHAPTER FOUR

PROTECTING AND PRESERVING WEALTH

RISK MANAGEMENT AND INSURANCE

Growing wealth involves not only maximizing gains but also safeguarding against potential losses. Risk management and insurance play pivotal roles in this pursuit, serving as protective shields against unforeseen adversities.

Understanding Risk: Risk is an inherent aspect of any investment or financial endeavor. It encompasses various factors, including market volatility, economic fluctuations, and individual circumstances. Recognizing and assessing different types of risk is fundamental to prudent financial planning.

Diversification as a Risk Management Tool: Diversifying investments across different asset classes and industries is a cornerstone of risk management. Spreading investments reduces the impact of potential losses from any single asset, mitigating overall portfolio risk. It's a strategy that balances risk while allowing for potential growth.

Insurance as a Risk Mitigation Strategy: Insurance serves as a vital component of risk management. It acts as a safety net, offering protection against unforeseen events such as accidents, illnesses, property damage, or legal liabilities. Health insurance, life insurance, auto insurance, home insurance, and liability coverage are among the various types available, each serving a specific purpose in shielding against potential financial setbacks.

Risk Assessment and Mitigation Planning: Assessing personal risk tolerance and financial circumstances guides the selection of appropriate insurance coverage. Analyzing potential risks and identifying coverage gaps ensures adequate protection. For instance, considering the impact of health emergencies, disability, or loss of income helps determine suitable health and disability insurance coverage.

Emergency Funds and Contingency Planning: Building emergency funds acts as another layer of risk management. These funds, typically three to six months' worth of living expenses, provide a financial cushion during unexpected situations, reducing the need to rely solely on insurance coverage.

Regular Reviews and Updates: Regularly reviewing insurance policies and reassessing risk exposure is crucial. Life changes, such as marriage, having children, career advancements, or acquiring new assets, may necessitate adjustments in insurance coverage to adequately protect against evolving risks.

Professional Guidance and Risk Assessment: Seeking guidance from financial advisors or insurance professionals aids in navigating the complexities of risk management. These professionals can conduct comprehensive risk assessments, recommend appropriate insurance products, and devise strategies tailored to individual risk profiles and financial goals.

In essence, risk management and insurance form essential components of a holistic wealth growth strategy. They act as protective measures, ensuring that while aiming for financial growth, individuals are also fortified against potential setbacks and unexpected challenges that could jeopardize their financial well-being. By integrating these elements into their financial plans, individuals can cultivate a more resilient and secure path towards wealth accumulation.

ESTATE PLANNING & WEALTH TRANSFER

Estate planning and wealth transfer encompass the strategic and meticulous orchestration of one's assets, ensuring their seamless transition to intended beneficiaries while optimizing tax efficiency and minimizing complications. At its core, estate planning is a comprehensive roadmap that encompasses not just the transfer of wealth but also considerations for healthcare directives, guardianship arrangements for dependents, and end-of-life wishes.

Central to estate planning is the creation of a will—a legal document that outlines how assets and properties are to be distributed upon the individual's passing. It delineates beneficiaries, designates an executor to oversee the estate's administration, and may include provisions for charitable donations or trusts. Crafting a will tailored to specific familial and financial circumstances is fundamental, as it not only ensures one's wishes are honored but also mitigates potential disputes among heirs.

Trusts are another pivotal aspect of estate planning, offering diverse structures that facilitate wealth transfer while providing control and protection over assets. Irrevocable trusts, for instance, can shield assets from estate taxes and creditors, while revocable living trusts allow for flexibility during the grantor's lifetime, often enabling seamless asset management and transfer without probate.

Furthermore, estate planning involves considerations for minimizing tax liabilities. Strategies such as gifting, setting up trusts, and utilizing tax-efficient accounts can help reduce the estate's tax burden. By leveraging exemptions and deductions available in estate tax laws, individuals can safeguard a larger portion of their wealth for future generations.

In addition to the financial aspects, healthcare directives play a crucial role in estate planning.

Advanced healthcare directives, including living wills and healthcare proxies, outline an individual's preferences regarding medical treatment in case of incapacitation. Assigning power of attorney for healthcare decisions ensures that trusted individuals can make medical choices aligned with the individual's wishes.

Succession planning for family businesses is also a vital component of estate planning. Establishing a clear roadmap for the transfer of ownership and management of the business ensures continuity and minimizes disruptions in operations while addressing the financial implications of the transition.

Moreover, regular review and updating of estate plans are essential. Changes in laws, financial circumstances, family dynamics, or personal preferences may necessitate revisions to the estate plan. Staying vigilant and adapting plans accordingly ensures their continued relevance and effectiveness.

In essence, estate planning and wealth transfer encompass a holistic approach to safeguarding assets, ensuring their efficient transfer to intended beneficiaries, and honoring an individual's wishes. By meticulously crafting a comprehensive estate plan, individuals not only secure their financial legacy but also provide clarity and protection for their loved ones amidst life's uncertainties.

PHILANTHROPY AND GIVING BACK

Philanthropy and giving back represent an integral facet of growing wealth beyond mere financial accumulation. It transcends the traditional notion of wealth, encompassing the enrichment of communities, fostering social impact, and leaving a legacy that extends far beyond monetary success.

At its essence, philanthropy embodies a spirit of generosity, compassion, and a profound desire to effect positive change. It's a conscious decision to leverage one's resources, whether financial, intellectual, or influential, to address societal issues, uplift underserved communities, and contribute to causes that resonate deeply.

The act of giving back goes beyond writing a check; it involves active engagement, empathy, and a genuine commitment to making a difference. It can take various forms, from supporting education initiatives and healthcare programs to championing environmental conservation or advocating for social justice causes. Whether through direct involvement in grassroots organizations or partnering with established philanthropic entities, individuals channel their resources toward initiatives aligned with their values and societal needs.

Moreover, philanthropy serves as a catalyst for personal growth and fulfillment. It fosters a sense of purpose and satisfaction derived from creating meaningful impacts in the lives of others. It provides a profound sense of connection and empathy, broadening perspectives and nurturing a deeper understanding of the interconnectedness of humanity.

For many, philanthropy is not only about giving during moments of abundance but integrating giving into their overall wealth-building strategy. It's an acknowledgment of the responsibility that comes with wealth, recognizing the capacity to effect positive change and influence systemic improvements in society.

The impact of philanthropy extends beyond immediate beneficiaries; it leaves a lasting legacy, inspiring future generations and setting an example of social responsibility. By instilling philanthropic values and practices, individuals not only leave a mark on society but also empower others to carry forth the torch of giving, perpetuating a culture of compassion and generosity.

In the realm of wealth growth, philanthropy stands as a testament to the holistic nature of abundance. It illustrates that true wealth encompasses not only financial prosperity but also the richness derived from giving, contributing, and leaving a positive imprint on the world—a legacy that transcends generations and echoes the values and beliefs held dear.

CHAPTER FIVE

NAVIGATING CHALLENGES

OVERCOMING FINANCIAL SETBACKS

Overcoming financial setbacks is an inherent part of the wealth-building journey, demanding resilience, adaptability, and a strategic approach. When confronted with such challenges, it's crucial to embrace a proactive mindset and adopt strategies that foster recovery and continued growth.

Firstly, acknowledge and assess the setback. This involves a candid evaluation of the situation, understanding the root causes, and assessing the extent of the impact. Whether it's a market downturn affecting investments, unexpected expenses, job loss, or business setbacks, comprehending the factors at play lays the groundwork for effective planning.

Next, establish a realistic action plan. Prioritize critical tasks such as managing immediate financial obligations, restructuring debts, or revising your budget. Taking swift and decisive action can mitigate the consequences and prevent the setback from exacerbating.

Maintaining a positive mindset amidst adversity is paramount. Understand that setbacks are temporary hurdles, not permanent roadblocks. Cultivating a resilient attitude enables the exploration of alternative solutions and keeps focus on long-term financial goals despite temporary setbacks.

Explore opportunities for generating income or cutting expenses. This might involve seeking additional sources of income, freelancing, or downsizing non-essential expenses. Being resourceful and adaptive in finding new revenue streams aids in stabilizing finances and accelerating recovery.

Utilize available resources and seek professional advice when necessary. Financial advisors or mentors can provide guidance and expertise in navigating challenging situations, offering tailored strategies to weather the setback and regain financial stability.

Revisit your financial goals and reassess your investment strategy. A setback might necessitate a reevaluation of risk tolerance, asset allocation, or long-term objectives. Adjusting investment portfolios or financial plans in alignment with revised goals can help recalibrate towards sustained growth.

Moreover, prioritize building an emergency fund for future resilience. Setting aside funds for unexpected expenses acts as a buffer against future setbacks, ensuring greater financial security and peace of mind.

Embrace the opportunity for personal growth and learning from setbacks. Each challenge presents a valuable lesson—be it in financial management, risk assessment, or resilience. Leveraging these experiences as learning opportunities strengthens financial acumen for future endeavors.

Finally, maintain perseverance and patience. Recovering from setbacks takes time and persistence. Celebrate small victories along the way and remain committed to your long-term financial aspirations.

In essence, overcoming financial setbacks requires a multifaceted approach encompassing strategic planning, adaptability, resilience, and a positive mindset. By implementing these strategies, individuals can not only navigate through setbacks but also emerge stronger and more resilient on their path to growing wealth.

PSYCHOLOGICAL BARRIERS TO WEALTH

Growing wealth involves not just financial strategies but also navigating psychological barriers that often hinder individuals from achieving their full financial potential. These barriers, deeply rooted in perceptions, behaviors, and emotions, can significantly impact one's ability to accumulate wealth.

1. Scarcity Mindset: One of the most prevalent barriers is the scarcity mindset, where individuals fixate on limitations rather than opportunities. This mindset fosters fear of taking risks, reluctance to invest, and a constant worry about potential losses. It perpetuates a cycle of scarcity, preventing individuals from seizing growth opportunities.

2. Fear of Failure: The fear of failure can paralyze decision-making, preventing individuals from taking calculated risks that could lead to wealth accumulation. This fear often stems from societal pressures, a fear of judgment, or a reluctance to step out of comfort zones. It results in missed opportunities and stagnation.

3. Instant Gratification vs. Delayed Gratification: The preference for instant gratification over delayed rewards can hinder wealth growth. A focus on immediate pleasures or spending habits without considering long-term consequences impedes the habit of saving and investing for the future.

4. Negative Money Scripts: Deeply ingrained beliefs about money, inherited from upbringing or past experiences, can create negative money scripts. These scripts might include beliefs that wealth is unattainable, money is inherently evil, or that one doesn't deserve financial success. These beliefs subconsciously influence financial decisions and limit wealth-building behaviors.

5. Lack of Financial Education: A lack of financial literacy can be a significant barrier. Without understanding basic financial concepts, individuals might feel overwhelmed, leading to avoidance or making uninformed decisions that hinder wealth growth.

6. Comfort with Status Quo: Complacency with one's current financial situation, even if it's suboptimal, can hinder wealth accumulation. Accepting mediocrity or feeling content with minimal progress can prevent individuals from seeking growth opportunities.

7. Emotional Biases: Emotions like greed, overconfidence, or fear can cloud judgment and lead to irrational financial decisions. Greed might lead to excessive risk-taking; overconfidence can result in overlooking risks, and fear can drive overly conservative decisions.

8. Social and Cultural Influences: Social pressures and cultural norms around money can significantly impact wealth-building efforts. Peer pressure to spend or live beyond one's means, or cultural stigmas associated with wealth, might hinder individuals from making sound financial decisions.

Overcoming these psychological barriers involves introspection, education, and a deliberate effort to reframe beliefs and behaviors around money. It requires developing a growth-oriented mindset, seeking financial education, challenging limiting beliefs, and embracing calculated risks aligned with financial goals. Breaking free from these barriers empowers individuals to cultivate healthy financial habits and unlock their full potential for wealth accumulation.

BUILDING RESILLENCE AND PERSISTENCE

Building resilience and persistence on the path to wealth is a testament to the unwavering commitment and steadfastness required to navigate the inevitable challenges and setbacks that arise along the journey. Resilience encompasses the ability to bounce back from adversity, while persistence embodies the determination to pursue goals despite obstacles.

At the core of building resilience and persistence lies the understanding that setbacks are not roadblocks but opportunities for growth. Resilient individuals perceive challenges as temporary detours rather than permanent defeats. They embrace failures as valuable lessons, extracting wisdom from each experience to refine their strategies and fortify their resolve. It's about maintaining a positive outlook amid adversity, recognizing that every setback is a stepping stone toward eventual success.

Cultivating resilience involves developing coping mechanisms and adaptive strategies to manage stress and adversity. This often includes fostering a strong support network of mentors, peers, or advisors who offer guidance, encouragement, and perspective during challenging times. It also entails cultivating emotional intelligence, understanding one's emotions, and channeling them into productive actions rather than being overwhelmed by them.

Persistence, on the other hand, is the unwavering commitment to staying the course despite obstacles. It's about setting long-term goals and pursuing them with tenacity, regardless of temporary setbacks or failures. Persistent individuals possess a resolute mindset, refusing to be deterred by initial setbacks or delays. They understand that success often requires time, effort, and a continuous willingness to adapt and evolve.

Building persistence involves fostering a strong sense of purpose and vision. When individuals are driven by a clear sense of purpose, setbacks become temporary deviations on the road to their ultimate destination. They remain focused on their long-term goals, adjusting their strategies while staying true to their vision.

Moreover, persistence is about maintaining discipline and consistency in actions. It's the daily commitment to taking small steps toward larger goals, even when progress seems slow or obstacles appear insurmountable. Consistency in effort, coupled with a belief in the ultimate outcome, forms the bedrock of persistence.

Ultimately, building resilience and persistence on the

path to wealth requires a combination of mental strength, adaptability, determination, and patience. It's the continuous cultivation of a mindset that embraces challenges as opportunities for growth and remains resolute in the pursuit of long-term goals, no matter the obstacles encountered along the way.

6

CHAPTER SIX

EMBRACING WEALTH

ACHIEVING FINANCIAL FREEDOM

Finally achieving financial freedom is akin to reaching the summit of a lifelong expedition, where the horizon expands beyond monetary measures to embrace a life liberated from financial constraints. It marks a culmination of disciplined efforts, strategic planning, and a mindset shift that transcends mere wealth accumulation. Financial freedom isn't solely about the numbers in one's bank account; it's about the empowerment that arises from having control over one's financial destiny.

At its core, financial freedom grants individuals the autonomy to make choices that align with their aspirations, values, and passions. It liberates from the shackles of financial stress, allowing for a life lived on one's terms. It's the ability to pursue endeavors not solely for monetary gain but for fulfillment, personal growth, and making a meaningful impact on the world.

Achieving financial freedom demands a steadfast commitment to disciplined financial habits and a proactive approach to wealth management. It

44

involves meticulous budgeting, prudent saving, and strategic investments that accumulate over time, compounding to create a robust financial foundation. This journey often requires sacrifices, delayed gratification, and a focus on long-term goals over immediate desires.

Moreover, financial freedom is about securing a sustainable and reliable income stream that isn't solely dependent on active labor. It involves creating passive income sources, such as investments, royalties, or businesses, that generate revenue independently, providing a consistent flow of funds to support one's lifestyle.

However, financial freedom isn't a static destination but an evolving state that adapts to changing circumstances and goals. It requires continuous learning, adaptation, and prudent decision-making to preserve and grow wealth. It's about safeguarding against unexpected challenges, ensuring financial resilience, and securing the future for oneself and future generations.

Beyond the tangible benefits, achieving financial freedom nurtures a sense of peace, security, and confidence. It offers the freedom to explore new horizons, pursue one's passions, and contribute to causes that resonate deeply. It fosters a mindset of abundance, gratitude, and the ability to leverage resources not just for personal gain but for the betterment of society.

In essence, finally achieving financial freedom represents a transformative journey, marked not only by monetary accomplishments but by the empowerment and liberation that arises from taking charge of one's financial destiny. It's a gateway to a life rich in possibilities, purpose, and profound fulfillment—a true testament to the realization of enduring wealth in its most holistic sense.

LIVING A FULFIILLING AND BALANCED LIFE

Living a fulfilling and balanced life, especially after achieving financial freedom, becomes the pinnacle of the journey. It transcends the realm of finances, encompassing holistic well-being across various dimensions of life.

Fulfillment emanates from aligning one's actions and choices with personal values, passions, and a sense of purpose. It's about finding meaning in everyday endeavors, cultivating deep and meaningful relationships, and nurturing personal growth. Achieving financial freedom offers the opportunity to direct time and energy toward these aspects, fostering a life of richness beyond monetary wealth.

A balanced life revolves around harmony among different spheres—personal, professional, social, and emotional. It entails setting boundaries and priorities, recognizing that wealth and success are facets of life but not the sole defining factors. It's the art of balancing work commitments with leisure, family time, personal hobbies, and self-care.

Financial freedom allows for the pursuit of experiences rather than mere possessions. It's about exploring the world, savoring diverse cultures, indulging in enriching experiences, and creating lasting memories. It's also about investing in personal growth—learning new skills, nurturing talents, and embarking on self-discovery journeys that contribute to personal fulfillment.

Additionally, a fulfilling life post-financial freedom often involves giving back to the community and making a positive impact. It's the joy derived from philanthropy, volunteering, or supporting causes that resonate deeply. It's the realization that true wealth lies not only in what one accumulates but also in what one contributes to the world.

Moreover, maintaining physical and mental well-being is integral to a balanced life. Financial freedom affords the resources and time to prioritize health—engaging in regular exercise, maintaining a nutritious diet, practicing mindfulness, and seeking mental tranquility. This balance is the cornerstone of sustaining a fulfilling life in the long run.

Ultimately, achieving financial freedom sets the stage for a life lived with intentionality and balance. It offers the freedom to design a life rich in purpose, experiences, relationships, personal growth, and well-being. It's about embracing the full spectrum of human existence, finding equilibrium amidst the complexities of life, and savoring the richness that arises from a life well-lived.

SUSTAINING AND SHARING YOUR WEALTH

Sustaining and sharing wealth, especially after achieving financial freedom, marks the transition from personal success to a legacy of impact and significance. It involves responsible stewardship of resources and a commitment to perpetuating wealth for future generations while also giving back to society.

Sustaining wealth entails prudent financial management and preserving assets for the long term. It involves a continued adherence to the principles that led to financial freedom—disciplined budgeting, wise investment choices, and prudent risk management. Moreover, it often involves estate planning and establishing structures that ensure the smooth transfer of wealth, minimizing tax liabilities and securing the financial well-being of heirs.

Beyond preservation, sharing wealth involves philanthropy, charitable giving, and contributing to causes that align with personal values. It's about using resources to effect positive change, whether through supporting education, healthcare, environmental conservation, or social initiatives. Financial freedom offers the means to make a meaningful impact, leaving a legacy that extends beyond material possessions.

Moreover, sharing wealth extends to imparting financial education and values to the next generation. It involves instilling a sense of responsibility, knowledge, and stewardship in heirs, ensuring they understand the value of wealth and the importance of contributing positively to society. Furthermore, sustaining and sharing wealth involves a mindset of abundance and a recognition that wealth is a tool for creating a better world. It's about fostering a culture of generosity, empathy, and social responsibility, leveraging resources to address systemic issues and drive positive change in communities.

However, this process is not without its challenges. Balancing the desire to sustain wealth for future generations while also making impactful contributions can require thoughtful consideration and strategic planning. Additionally, ensuring that charitable efforts are effective and aligned with one's values demands careful evaluation and collaboration with reputable organizations or initiatives.

In essence, sustaining and sharing wealth after achieving financial freedom embodies a transition from personal success to a legacy of significance. It's about fostering a cycle of prosperity that extends beyond oneself, leaving an indelible mark on the world through responsible stewardship, impactful giving, and empowering future generations to carry forward a legacy of positive change.

CONCLUSION

The journey towards financial freedom, sustaining wealth, and sharing abundance mirrors the ethos of 'The Wealth Train.' Just as the book encapsulates a holistic approach to wealth, these concepts intertwine to paint a complete picture of prosperity, stewardship, and purposeful living.

Consider Warren Buffett, whose prudent investments and commitment to long-term value creation exemplify the principles of sustaining wealth. He diversified Berkshire Hathaway's portfolio, building a conglomerate that spans industries, ensuring sustained growth over decades.

Similarly, the Gates Foundation embodies sharing wealth with a focus on eradicating diseases, improving education, and alleviating poverty. Bill and Melinda Gates' commitment to giving back showcases how financial freedom allows for impactful philanthropy, leaving a lasting imprint on society.

'The Wealth Train' embodies these ideals by offering a comprehensive journey toward financial empowerment. Its chapters on cultivating a wealth mindset mirror the discipline needed to sustain wealth, just as individuals like Elon Musk, through his resilience and innovation, have sustained multiple ventures, pushing the boundaries of entrepreneurship.

Moreover, the book's sections on balanced living resonate with individuals like Oprah Winfrey, who, after attaining financial freedom, focused on personal growth, philanthropy, and fostering meaningful connections.

The concept of sharing wealth, as explored in 'The Wealth Train,' aligns with figures like Mark Zuckerberg, who pledged a significant portion of his wealth toward charitable causes while continuously growing his personal fortune through Facebook.

In conclusion, 'The Wealth Train' encapsulates the holistic journey of financial empowerment, reflecting the intertwined aspects of financial freedom, sustaining wealth, and sharing abundance. It draws inspiration from real-life exemplars who've navigated this terrain, providing a roadmap for readers to cultivate a mindset, build a sustainable financial future, and make a meaningful impact on the world—ultimately embodying the essence of prosperity beyond mere monetary measures.

ABOUT THE AUTHOR

David Mark is a visionary author whose passion for empowering individuals to navigate the pathways of financial empowerment and holistic abundance shines through his writing. With a keen eye for insightful narratives and a knack for distilling complex concepts into relatable wisdom, David Mark has emerged as a guiding voice in the realm of personal finance and wealth creation.

Drawing from a diverse tapestry of experiences, David brings a unique perspective to the subject of wealth management, emphasizing not only the strategies for financial success but also the deeper significance of a balanced, purpose-driven life.

His commitment to cultivating a wealth mindset, fostering sustainable prosperity, and advocating for the sharing of abundance echoes in his works, inspiring readers to embark on transformative journeys toward financial independence and personal fulfillment.

Through his literary endeavors, David Mark endeavors to ignite the flames of possibility within his readers, equipping them with the tools, insights, and inspiration to embark on their own transformative quests toward a life of enduring wealth and significance.